DATE DUE

PRINTED IN U.S.A.

Making Choices
with FRIENDS

By Diane Lindsey Reeves

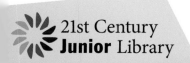
21st Century
Junior Library

Published in the United States of America by
Cherry Lake Publishing
Ann Arbor, Michigan
www.cherrylakepublishing.com

Reading Adviser: Marla Conn MS. Ed., Literacy specialist, Read-Ability, Inc.

Photo Credits: Cover, © Gagliardi Images; page 4, © verandah; page 6, © Pressmaster; page 8, © sirtravelalot; page 10, © Robert Kneschke; page 12, © Veronica Louro; page 14, © Ilike; page 16, © wavebreakmedia; page 18, © Monkey Business Images; page 20, © Monkey Business Images. *Source: Shutterstock.*

Library of Congress Cataloging-in-Publication Data
CIP data has been filed and is available at catalog.loc.gov.

Cherry Lake Publishing would like to acknowledge the work of The Partnership for 21st Century Skills.
Please visit *www.p21.org* for more information.

Printed in the United States of America.

CONTENTS

5 **Friends Are Fun**

11 **Let's Play**

17 **Choose Good Friends**

22 My Smart Choices

23 Glossary

24 Index

24 About the Author

Friends are always happy to see each other.

Friends Are Fun

Hello, friend! Having friends is so much fun. You have someone to play with. You have someone to talk to. You have someone to tell silly jokes to.

The best way to *have* a friend is to *be* a friend. How do you be a friend? Treat people the way you want to be treated. This is called the Golden Rule. And it works!

My Choice!

- Treat friends how I want to be treated
- Be **bossy** and mean

Friends like to talk to each other.

Friends are **friendly**. They smile and say hello. They ask how you are doing.

Friends talk to each other. They also **listen** to each other. Listening shows that you care about someone.

Talking and listening. This is how how friends get to know each other. They discover they like to do some of the same things.

Do you greet your friends with a smile? Do you talk *and* listen to them?

My Choice!

- Be friendly to my friends
- Do all the talking and don't listen

You can count on friends for a helping hand.

Friends **celebrate** good times together. Friends **share** birthdays and holidays. They make them extra fun.

Friends are happy when good things happen. You got an A on your test? Hurray! Your team won the game? Yippee!

Friends stick together in bad times too. Like when they make mistakes. Or get sick.

Can your friends count on you to be a good friend?

My Choice!

- Be a good friend all the time
- Only be a good friend in good times

It is fun to play with friends.

Let's Play

One thing all friends like to do is play. Good friends play nicely together. They often enjoy playing the same types of games.

Sometimes your friend gets to pick what to play. Sometimes you do. Taking turns is **fair**. It keeps everyone happy.

What games do you like to play with your friends? Are you careful to take turns?

My Choice!

- Play nice and take turns
- Only play what you want to play

Sometimes it is hard to share toys.

Good friends are good about sharing. But you don't have to share everything you own. Some of your toys are just for you to play with. Put them away when a friend comes over.

Other toys you are happy to share. Remember, sharing lasts just for a little while. Your friend will give your toys back.

Do you share your toys? Are you careful when you play with your friends' toys?

My Choice!

- I share with my friends
- I am **selfish** with my toys

No one likes to be left out.

Friends include other people when they play. It is no fun to be left out.

Is there a new kid at school? It is extra nice to include new kids. Is someone all alone? Invite that person to play with you. Including others is a good way to make new friends.

Do you include others when you play?

My Choice!

- I include other kids when I play
- I don't care if other kids are left out

Friends help each other out.

Choose Good Friends

Not everyone can be your friend. Some children are **bullies**. They boss people around. They are mean. They cause trouble. It is best to stay away from people like that. Is someone acting like a bully to you or your friend? Tell an adult!

Choose friends who bring out the best in you. Good friends help you be good, too.

My Choice!

- Choose good friends
- Choose friends who are mean to others

Gossip is never a good idea.

There is some good **advice** that friends follow. This is how it goes:

If you can't say something nice, say nothing at all.

Gossip is talking about other people. It can get mean really fast. It can hurt people's feelings.

Good friends don't gossip. They only say nice things about their friends.

My Choice!

- Say nice things about my friends
- Talk about friends behind their backs

Life is more fun with friends!

Some people have lots of friends. Some people choose just a few. It doesn't matter how many you have. What matters is how you treat them. And how they treat you.

True friends make everything more fun. Friends care about each other. They **trust** each other to be kind and helpful.

Have you been a good friend today?

My Choice!

- Make good friends
- Don't make friends

MY SMART CHOICES

Write a story about two different days. One day you make smart choices with your friends. The other day you don't. How are the two days different? Which day did you enjoy the most?

GLOSSARY

advice (uhd-VISE) wise suggestion about what to do

bossy (BAWS-ee) telling other people what to do; always trying to get your own way

bullies (BUL-eez) people who frighten or pick on someone smaller or weaker than they are

celebrate (SEL-uh-brate) to do something special to mark a happy event

fair (FAIR) balanced, equal for both people

friendly (FREND-lee) warm, kind, or helpful; acting like a friend

gossip (GAH-sip) to talk about another person when they aren't there

listen (LIS-uhn) to pay attention when someone is talking to you

selfish (SEL-fish) only interested in your own needs or wishes; not interested in sharing

share (SHAIR) to do together; also, to let someone use a toy or other belonging

trust (TRUHST) to believe someone is honest and reliable

INDEX

A
advice, 19

B
bullies, 17

C
celebrate, 9

F
fair, 11

G
Golden Rule, 5
gossip, 18, 19

H
house, playing, 11

M
My Choice, 5, 7, 9, 11,
    13, 15, 17, 18, 21
My Smart Choices, 22

P
pet doctor 11

S
school, playing 11
selfish, 13
sharing, 13
superheroes, 11

T
taking turns, 11

ABOUT THE AUTHOR

When Diane Lindsey Reeves isn't writing children's books, she chooses to play with her four grandchildren. She lives in Cary, North Carolina, and Washington, D.C.